PILGRIM YEAR

STEVE BELL

NOVALIS

© 2018 Steve Bell

Cover design and layout: Audrey Wells
Cover image: Roberta Landreth | Treehouse Design | designbyroberta.com

Published by Novalis

Publishing Office
10 Lower Spadina Avenue, Suite 400
Toronto, Ontario, Canada
M5V 2Z2

Head Office
4475 Frontenac Street
Montréal, Québec, Canada
H2H 2S2

www.novalis.ca

Library and Archives Canada Cataloguing in Publication

Bell, Steve, 1960-, author
        Pilgrim year / Steve Bell.
Contents: Volume 7. Ordinary time.
ISBN 978-2-89688-607-4 (v. 7 : softcover).

        1. Church year. I. Title.

BV30.B45 2018   263'.9   C2018-902326-0

Printed in Canada.

We acknowledge the support of the Government of Canada.

5   4   3   2   1   22   21   20   19   18

TABLE OF CONTENTS

INTRODUCTION

If you have acquired this book on its own, I hope you will be pleased to discover that it is one of seven books in a series that I have written reflecting on the rich tradition of the Church calendar year. The entire collection includes brief volumes on the seasons of Advent, Christmas, Epiphany, Lent, Holy Week, Easter and Ordinary Time.

Together, these recurring seasons, with their remembrances, fasts and feasts, retell and reharrow the living story of God and God's good creation – a story that has been entrusted to the Church; a story that often runs as a counter-narrative to stories broadly told in the wider culture. We must not be naive about such things, for stories really do matter. They fashion a rich bed of receptive imagination from which all manner of possibilities are either opened up or closed down. Indeed, if one wants to know the cause of the inspiring and/or bewildering behaviours of any given individual or culture, one need only investigate the foundational stories they tell.

Certainly, stories that tell of a random and meaningless universe will produce a different culture than stories of an enchanted, meaning-drenched cosmos. The radical capitalist story of human relationships necessarily playing out as a blood sport of self-interested individuals in a zero-sum game produces a different result than the story of a supra-abundant universe created in the image of the Triune God whose very being is one of dynamic relationality and mutual, self-donating love. Consider the stories behind popular reality shows such as *The Apprentice* and *Survivor*, where there is only one winner and many losers and in which every relationship is eventually sacrificed on the altar of self-interest. Compare them with the gospel stories, which tell of the God of creation emptying himself for the flourishing of all. One begins to grasp that such stories are so much more than pleasing fancies to while away our leisure hours. Some stories enrich and enliven. Some, quite frankly, are dangerous.

The Church tells and retells her sacred stories year after year, much as a mother to her children who ask for the same stories night after night. And like any good child's tale, they continue to reward well into adulthood. Each time we rehearse and reharrow these stories, we unearth something new precisely because there is so much more to receive, but also because our capacity to receive has deepened.

We Christians are many things, but for sure we are *keepers of The Story*. We tend it like a fire in the darkest of nights, and we live by its blaze and glory during the day. We should not be scandalized if it sometimes harmonizes with stories from other cultures or faiths, because if indeed the world is "charged with the grandeur of God" which will "flame out like shining from shook foil" (as Gerard Manley Hopkins, one of our finer poets, has said), then we should be rather surprised if it didn't.

I have pilgrimed through these stories my entire life and I feel like I am only starting to know them. But to the degree that I have absorbed them as a living tradition, they have fashioned in me a unified mind, body and soul capable of loving God and loving all that God loves.

Let me take a stab at summarizing the tale of which each individual story of the Pilgrim Year is an illuminating piece. This is the best I can do right now, halfway through my 58th year. I hope that in five years it will develop and deepen some... and five years after that... and after that...

God is love. We have come from God and we are returning to God. All that is, is God's good idea, bears God's imprint and character, and radiates God's life.

God sustains all.

We have been made for union with God and with each other.

Humans in particular have been given the charge to steward creation and serve as its priest, gathering all creation in one voice in praise to the glory of our Maker.

Though dimly perceived because of sinful self-will and self-orientation, we yet live in a meaning-drenched universe.

Because we come from God and are returning to God, the Christian life is essentially a pilgrimage after the One who has both made a way and by whose light we can see the way.

HOW TO USE THIS BOOK

I've assembled the thoughts, prayers, poems and songs in this series as a companion guide for those seeking a deeper encounter with the spiritual tradition of the Christian calendar year.

The seven volumes in this series are not intended to be a daily devotional, as many of the reflections are not associated with a specific date; rather, each chapter highlights a particular nuance of the season that I have found worth reflecting on. Whenever a reflection is associated with a particular date, such as a saint's day or a fixed feast, this will be indicated under the chapter heading.

Read in sequence, hop around, read daily or all at once. It doesn't matter. Each chapter has a stand-alone quality that can be accessed without reference to the others.

Because the printed page is not capable of audio or video, we've created a companion website to this book where you can find the audio (songs) and visual (video) components associated with each chapter. Simply go to **www.pilgrimyear.com/songs** and click on the chapter heading you want to read: you will find those items there.

Because most chapters end with a song, you may want to find the song on the website first, listen to it once or twice, then read the chapter before listening again. Devotional songs have a way of both tilling the soil and setting the dye. It's best to receive them without analysis; they do their own work in their own way.

Finally, this series by no means attempts a comprehensive look at this rich tradition. I come to it late and am a novice myself. All I can do is leave a trail of bread crumbs to the grottos and vistas I have found. Hopefully, these pages will whet your imagination and draw you into your own pilgrimage.

To access the songs and videos
associated with these reflections, visit:

www.pilgrimyear.com/songs

Like a great waterwheel, the liturgical [Christian calendar] year goes on relentlessly irrigating our soul, softening the ground of our hearts, nourishing the soil of our lives until the seed of the word of God itself begins to grow in us, comes to fruit in us, ripens us in the spiritual journey of a lifetime.[1]

Joan Chittister

---

1   Joan Chittister, *The Liturgical Year: The Spiraling Adventure of the Spiritual Life* (Thomas Nelson, 2010).

LOVING THE DAILY DIVINE: INTRODUCTION TO ORDINARY TIME

Remain within the world of which you're made.
Call nothing common in the earth or air,
Accept it all and let it be for good.[2]

Malcolm Guite

Finally, we come to the last and longest season of the Christian year – Ordinary Time.

In many traditions, there are two seasons of Ordinary Time: one shorter season between Epiphany and Lent, and then a longer one, which this collection celebrates. Given the assumption that many readers of these pages are new to the Christian calendar tradition, I've chosen to keep it simple. We'll explore from the end of the Easter season around mid-May to the beginning of Advent in late November. In

---

2   Excerpt from the poem "Singing Bowl," in Malcolm Guite, *The Singing Bowl* (Canterbury Press, 2013), xv.

truth, the Christian calendar has several varieties and complexities I've not addressed, but which you will discover if you become a worshipping member of a faith community that attends to the tradition in one of its forms.

Ordinary Time, in general, offers a bit of a breather. It does contain significant feasts (Trinity Sunday, the Transfiguration, All Saints, and Christ the King) and saints' days to be celebrated, but it has much less drama than the other seasons. It has a more even keel and offers a chance to integrate the mysteries we encounter throughout the rest of the year.

It is during Ordinary Time that we attend to the holiness of our daily lives. We began by passing through Advent, where we considered the mystery of the human person, whose dignity is to accept the invitation to participate in the drama of salvation as maternal spouse of God, co-operating to bring Christ's life to the world. We then celebrated Christmas, where we apprehended the humble incarnation of the cosmos' Creator and reflected on the astonishing humanity of Jesus. In the season of Epiphany, we meditated on the miracles and events that revealed Jesus' divinity, and we came to understand the two natures (human and divine) of Christ, to whom our souls are wed. During Lent, we pondered the devastation wrought by our infidelities and the myriad inordinate attachments and desires that draw our affections away from our Lord. Then, during Holy Week, we walked alongside Jesus to the cross, where he assumed and redeemed those devastations so that we might again truly and freely love as well as knowing we are beloved by God. Eastertide was a sustained reflection on the miracle of resurrection and the eternally evergreen life on offer through Christ's victory over death. Now we come to Ordinary Time.

The very sound of the words 'Ordinary Time' seems a letdown after the drama that preceded it. The word 'ordinary' suggests the commonplace, uninteresting and featureless. It can describe a person with no special merit or distinction. But if we simply replace the word 'ordinary' with 'daily', a new appreciation becomes possible. For Ordinary Time is the season in which we come to realize the astonishing *holiness* of our daily lives as a consequence of all we have previously considered. Here, we begin to understand with joy that the daily is impregnated with the divine.

The first Sunday of Ordinary Time (if we start right after the Easter season) is Trinity Sunday. Although it doesn't get much press compared with days like Christmas or Easter, I contend that Trinity Sunday is the highest and most magnificent peak of illumination on the landscape of the Church year. Everything that has preceded it points towards, and is a mere foothill relative to, this great revelation. Christ's birth, life, death and resurrection all conspire to bring us to this moment when we see the community (Father, Son, Spirit) that is God's eternal love and life, for which we have been redeemed and into which we have been wholeheartedly invited. From this dizzying summit, we look down on the plains of daily-ness and see it both bathed and infused with the light of God's intrinsic mutuality, goodness and love. The whole point of attending to the Christian year is to come to this moment where we awaken to the mystery of a daily-ness which, far from ordinary, radiates back to God's own being. Ironically, we can come to know in our bones that nothing conceived and sustained under God's gaze is ordinary.

Novelist Walker Percy, in his essay "The Holiness of the Ordinary," reflects on how the Christian spiritual tradition confers "the highest significance upon the ordinary things of this world: bread, wine, water, touch, breath, words, talking, listening." A world which is itself a sacrament and a mystery.[3]

Recently, I was asked to contribute a song to a compilation CD. It wasn't a "Christian" project, so the assumption was that I'd submit something that wouldn't be, as it were, *too Christian*. Producer Murray Pulver and I sat down to write a song that simply celebrated ordinariness (daily-ness) as it comes to us: as the *advent*-ure that it is, which of course, at the end of this season, leads right back into Advent again.

---

3   Walker Percy, *Signposts in a Strange Land* (Picador, 1991), 369.

BRING IT ON

by Murray Pulver and Steve Bell

Waking to familiar news
Summer's gone, long gone
Some are nursing winter's blues
Bring it on, bring it on

Crumble of snow beneath the feet
Shivering fingers, winter's cheek
True north time is bittersweet
Bring it on, bring it on

Not the youth I used to be
Marveling how the time has gone
Yet I've never felt so free
Bring it on, bring it on

Less to conquer, less to do
Less inclined to suffer fools
Just happy to grow old with you
Bring it on, bring it on

Fumbling forward on the way
Why regret, just journey on
In the end it's all okay
Bring it on, bring it on
Bring it on, bring it on

*Listen to the above song at www.pilgrimyear.com/songs:
Ordinary Time Chapter One.*

2

TRINITY SUNDAY

If the triune God is the source of all being...
we must suppose that all being will in some way
reflect the one who made it and holds it in being.[4]

Colin E. Gunton

I f I were granted authority to dictate such things, I would
declare Trinity Sunday the high holyday of the Christian
year. For it seems to me that every lesser epiphany we
celebrate in our traditional remembrances is a hint and a
signpost to the great revelation of God as Trinity: Father,
Son, and Holy Spirit – what the great Scottish theologian
James B. Torrance calls God's "Being-in-communion."[5]

Trinity Sunday is the first Sunday after Pentecost in
the Western liturgical calendar and the actual Sunday of

---

4   Colin E. Gunton, *The One, the Three and the Many: God, Creation and the Culture of Modernity* (Cambridge University Press, 1993), 145.

5   James B. Torrance, *Worship, Community and the Triune God of Grace* (IVP Press, 1997), 35.

Pentecost in the Eastern tradition. On this day we celebrate the doctrine of the Trinity and its profound implications. For we understand that God is indeed *one,* not as a tree is one, but rather as a forest is one. If it is true that we have been made in the image of God, then this is an epiphany (aha! moment) that changes everything.

From this lofty height, this Everest of revelation, we look upon and begin to apprehend the profound dignity of human persons made in the image of this God. We see, in fact, that the whole cosmos reflects this Being-in-communion. Even if we can only partially apprehend this revelation, it should stagger the mind with awe and clarify our vision to see the inherent sacredness of all things. Why? Because this divine relationality of the Trinity articulates, sustains and gives meaning to all of creation.

This same revelation also sobers us to the calamitous tragedy that is sin. For sin is, at its basic level, the denial of our truest selves. Sin is our failure to live out our given nature as image bearers of this divine mutuality (love), revealed in Jesus and made known to us by the inspiration of the Holy Spirit. Sin is the avowal of the self alone. Salvation, by contrast, is concord and communion.

I once attended a songwriters' retreat where Gary Dedo, then senior editor of InterVarsity Press, spoke to us about the mystery of God's Being-in-communion. We make the mistake, he challenged, of asking God the wrong questions. We ask *what, where* and *when* questions, when we should be asking *who*: *Who* are you? If we get the *who* question wrong, Gary insisted, we get all the other questions wrong as well.

A few days later, I dreamed I was standing on the edge of a cliff looking out over an ominous and eternal abyss. Cupping my hands over my mouth I called out, "Who are you?" and listened as my question reverberated into the deep. I stood for the longest time, waiting for a response until I determined none would come. As I turned to walk sadly away, I detected a faint voice on the wind with the reply "Who are *you*?" My sadness deepened because I didn't know.

Years later, I was performing on stage with my go-to piano player, Mike Janzen. We were having one of those rare evenings when everything was working perfectly. The sound was perfect, the audience was electrified and the orchestra members we were performing with were all intensely engaged. It was the kind of night that musicians live for. At the end of the closing song – a dramatic, high-energy piece – Mike took an extended piano solo. Although I was accustomed to his stellar performances, something on this night was elevated far beyond my expectations. He was dialled in and playing like I'd never heard before.

As his fingers flew over the keys, Mike's eyes locked onto mine while I was concentrating as hard as I could to make sure everything I played on my guitar enhanced and fuelled his own playing. Together we entered into an unrehearsed yet consuming musical dialogue until I realized that as intently as I was investing in Mike, he was doing the exact thing in return. No one was leading. The best words I can think of to describe what was happening was that we were mutually-othering. In other words, we were each pouring into the other, mindless of the self.

Suddenly, the whole scene froze in time and space. There seemed to be no movement, no sound, except a voice welling up inside me, saying, "Pay attention. *This* is who I Am." Everything remained silent and still as the impact of those words sank in. The scene in front of me returned to full motion. It was all I could do to remain sitting upright. Unaccustomed to such presence, my body wanted to utterly collapse. I was a mess for weeks afterward.

Mutual-othering: *This* Is Who I Am

How can I unpack this experience in a practical way? The format of a short devotional seems inadequate, even if I had the capacity to comprehend and articulate such mysteries. Fellow pilgrims who would like to pursue this idea further may want to read Colin Gunton's excellent book *The One, the Three, and the Many: God, Creation and the Culture of Modernity*.

Another excellent resource is *Worship, Community and the Triune God of Grace* by James B. Torrance, who writes: "God, who has His loving Being-in-communion… has, in the freedom of His love, created us and redeemed us that we might find our true being in communion with Him and one another."[6]

Just how far does the selfless "othering" of God extend? And to what degree does that inform our own understanding of what it means to be made in the image and likeness of God and to order our affairs accordingly? I suspect the answer would take us way out of our comfort zones. But honestly, what do we have to lose? Perhaps only the alienated and isolated self. What do we have to gain? Perhaps everything.

Given the current precariousness of our social and environmental relationships wrought by the Western cult of radical individualism, we may do well to return to the *who* question and wait on the One who can answer.

Perhaps the best accompaniment to our waiting is doxology:

PRAISE THE FATHER

music and lyrics by Gord Johnson

Who is the One to whom you belong
Who in your weakness has made you strong
Who fills your heart with joyful song
It is the Lord your God

---

6   Torrance, *Worship, Community and the Triune God of Grace*, 35.

Praise the Father, praise the Son
Praise the Spirit, three in One
Who was and is and is to come
All praise and honour and glory and power
O praise His name forever

Who is the One who for you died
Was mocked and spat at and crucified
Who rose from the dead and is glorified
It is the Lord your God

Praise the Father, praise the Son
Praise the Spirit, three in One
Who was and is and is to come
All praise and honour and glory and power
O praise His name forever

Who is the One whom with you will be
From highest mountain to darkest valley
Who is the One whom in you dwells
It is the Lord your God

Praise the Father, praise the Son
Praise the Spirit, three in One
Who was and is and is to come
All praise and honour and glory and power
O praise His name forever

Listen to the above song at www.pilgrimyear.com/songs:
Ordinary Time Chapter Two.

3

THE NATIVITY OF
JOHN THE BAPTIST

June 24

Indeed John was the morning-star,
for just as the morning star precedes the sun,
so he preceded Christ;
for he preached Christ first.[7]

William Durand of Mende (1230–1296 CE)

The Nativity of John the Baptist is one of only three feasts wherein the Church celebrates the birth (rather than the death) of a saint and as such fulfills the prophetic words of the Angel Gabriel to John's father Zechariah that "many will rejoice in his birth" (Luke 1:14). Traditionally, it has been the death of any given saint that has warranted

---

7   William Durand, *Rationale Divinorum Officiorum*, 7, 28. Cited in Gregory Dipippo, "Liturgical Notes on the Nativity of St. John the Baptist," *New Liturgical Movement: Sacred Liturgy & Liturgical Arts,* http://www.newliturgicalmovement.org/2015/06/liturgical-notes-on-nativity-of-st-john.html.

celebration, since death symbolizes their, and our, true birth into glory. However, John's significance in the unfolding drama of salvation is evident in that his nativity is uniquely celebrated alongside those of Jesus and Mary. The three feasts together have evolved beautifully over the centuries to fuel the devout imagination with rich symbolism: John, the morning star; Mary, the dawn; and Jesus, the rising sun in whom "the splendour of the Father appeared."[8]

We don't know the actual dates of either birth, but soon after the Church settled on December 25 to commemorate the birth of Christ, John's nativity was set six months before, to line up with the claim in Luke's Gospel that John's mother, Elizabeth, was six months pregnant at the time of the Annunciation (1:36). If it be only an accident that in the northern hemisphere, the nativity of John falls at the summer solstice, when the days begin to shorten, and that Jesus' nativity falls at the winter solstice, when the days begin to lengthen, then it is a happy accident. For John, in relationship to Jesus, instinctively knew that "he [Jesus] must increase, but I [John] must decrease" (John 3:30). If John the Baptist is the dimming light of the Old Covenant, and Jesus is the ascending light of the new, then this is the stuff of poets.

John the Baptist was a favourite Bible character of my childhood for a couple of reasons. First, being reared in the Baptist Church, I can't be faulted for my smug childhood

---

8   Durand, *Rationale Divinorum Officiorum.*

assumption that he was, after all, one of us. I can still re-member the disappointment I felt when I realized my mis-understanding. But more interestingly, John was a spectacle, and what child doesn't love a spectacle? I was fascinated by this thundering wild man, emerging out of the barren desert wearing a coarse camel-hair tunic and eating only locusts and wild honey. Weary of the wickedness that brought so much suffering to so many, he waved his hairy fists as he warned those who would exploit others not to trust in their spiritual heritage, calling some vipers and threatening the destruction of others. He didn't hesitate to rebuke the wily scoundrel and Roman comprador King Herod, and paid the price with his own imprisonment and eventual beheading. He promised a mighty messiah to come who would not mess around with water for baptisms, but who would baptize with fire. No doubt I would have been one of the awestruck many that flocked to the desert to see him.

At this point I can't help but humorously recall my son Jesse at around age ten being transferred to a different school at which my wife, Nanci, was a new teacher. Having no prior history with the other kids, I suppose he figured he needed to establish himself with a spectacle of some sort. Nanci was on recess duty when she noticed a shouting mob of kids at the far side of the schoolyard. Assuming a fight, she pushed her way into the middle to discover our son eating a mouthful of worms, to the squealing delight and disgust of the other boys and girls. My son knew how to draw a crowd. Had Jesse had a burning message in his heart, he might have started a movement after that stunt.

But John did have a message. He knew the promised Messiah was at hand and that things were about to change radically. No doubt John's hopes for Israel's salvation were comingled with her nationalistic aspirations after centuries of harsh and humiliating foreign rule. Quite possibly he anticipated, much like the prophets of religious extremism today, a militaristic salvation that first required a fiery purging of impurities and a renewed adherence to purity codes. As loudly and as spectacularly as he could, he heralded what he knew:

> Prepare the way of the Lord,
> make his paths straight.
> Every valley shall be filled,
> and every mountain and hill shall be made low,
> and the crooked shall be made straight,
> and the rough ways made smooth;
> and all flesh shall see the salvation of God.
> (Luke 3:4-6)

One cannot help but notice in John's message a familial resemblance to his Aunt Mary's Magnificat:

> He has shown strength with his arm;
> he has scattered the proud in the thoughts
>   of their hearts.
> He has brought down the powerful from their thrones,

and lifted up the lowly;
he has filled the hungry with good things,
and sent the rich away empty... (Luke 1:51-53)

Both John and Mary intuited that the salvation of God would entail a cataclysmic levelling of the playing field. They were right in that Jesus would mightily upset the apple cart, but who could have predicted he would do so by preaching forgiveness for the sinner, love of the enemy and inclusion for the excluded? Who would have predicted a saviour who would heal the enemy's children, feast with traitors and accept the affections of the marginalized and despised? Who could have anticipated a Christ who would eventually hang on a cross in solidarity with the rejected and God-forsaken? Jesus' teachings and manner were so radically counter-intuitive to what John expected that while imprisoned by Herod, he began to second guess what he thought he knew at Jesus' baptism. He sent messengers to ask Jesus, "Are you the one who was to come? Or should we expect someone else?" (Luke 7:20).

Jesus replied: "Go and tell John what you have seen and heard: the blind receive their sight, the lame walk, the lepers are cleansed, the deaf hear, the dead are raised, the poor have good news brought to them. And blessed is anyone who takes no offence at me" (7:22-23).

At this point, John falls silent and is not heard from again.

It is one thing to announce God. It is quite another to let God be God. Perhaps the greatness of John, that Jesus was only too happy to acknowledge, was in part that he did just that, symbolically bowing out of history so that God could renew it. It was John, the last great prophet of the Old Covenant and the old paradigm, who heralded the new. Then, he simply and humbly got out of the way. "He must increase, and I must decrease."

There is a lovely tradition, still practised over much of Europe, of lighting bonfires on the eve of the Nativity of John the Baptist. John was a forerunner of the true light that enlightens every woman and man, much the same as an evening bonfire is a forerunner of the rising sun. The greatness of John (Yohanan means 'God is gracious') is not so much who he was, but who he was pointing towards.

On the day of John's birth, his father, Zechariah, to whom the Angel Gabriel appeared, intuited the graciousness of God in his most sublime canticle:

"And you, child, will be called the prophet of
    the Most High;
for you will go before the Lord to prepare his ways,
to give knowledge of salvation to his people
by the forgiveness of their sins.
By the tender mercy of our God,
the dawn from on high will break upon us,
to give light to those who sit in darkness and
    in the shadow of death,

to guide our feet into the way of peace."
(Luke 1:76-79)

I will think of these things the next time my wife and I light a fire in our backyard. In the darkness of our own days, may we, like John, give way to the true light and way of peace that only Christ can illumine.

THE ANGEL GABRIEL

music and lyrics by Jim Croegaert

I have not seen the angel Gabriel
Standing at the right side of the altar
Saying that important line of angels
"Do not be afraid."

I have not heard the angel Gabriel
Telling me my prayer has been answered
That my heart's desire has been granted
And my wife will bear a son

But I have been answered
And I have been promised
In words that cannot be spoken
And the tender mercies of our God
Have caused the rising son to shine upon us
To guide our feet unto the path of peace

I was not there when the angel Gabriel
Visited the village of Nazareth
Home of a young maiden he addressed
As the highly favored one

I did not hear the angel Gabriel
Promise what could not be imagined
Answered by a faith without fathom
"Let what you have said be done."

But I have been answered
And I have been promised
In words that cannot be spoken
And the tender mercies of our God
Have caused the rising son to shine upon us
To guide our feet unto the path of peace

*Listen to the above song at pilgrimyear.com/songs:
Ordinary Time Chapter Three.*

THE FEAST OF
THE TRANSFIGURATION OF JESUS
August 6

...this blazing fire burns only to purify,
to make our robes as white as those of Jesus,
to free us from our little attempts to tame God.[9]

Fred Gaiser

Every time I sit down to write a chapter for these pages, my concern is that I will not have enough to say. Inevitably, however, after a modest amount of research and reflection, I realize the result will be quite the opposite. For when we attempt to articulate divine mysteries, no words are adequate and no number of words is enough. This is why

---

9   Fred Gaiser, "Commentary on Psalm 50:1-6," Working Preacher blog (February 15, 2015), https://www.workingpreacher.org/preaching. aspx?commentary_id=2350.

we resort to poetry if we even hope to draw close enough to see "the Love that dances at the heart of things."

The account of Jesus' transfiguration that today's feast celebrates is a case in point:

TRANSFIGURATION

by Malcolm Guite

For that one moment, 'in and out of time',
On that one mountain where all moments meet,
The daily veil that covers the sublime
In darkling glass fell dazzled at his feet.
There were no angels full of eyes and wings
Just living glory full of truth and grace.
The Love that dances at the heart of things
Shone out upon us from a human face
And to that light the light in us leaped up,
We felt it quicken somewhere deep within,
A sudden blaze of long-extinguished hope
Trembled and tingled through the tender skin.
Nor can this blackened sky, this darkened scar
Eclipse that glimpse of how things really are.[10]

It's worth reading the story of the transfiguration in all three synoptic gospels, stories that vary only slightly in certain details: Matthew 17:1-9, Mark 9:2-8 and Luke

---

10   Malcolm Guite, *Sounding the Seasons: Seventy Sonnets for the Christian Year* (Canterbury Press, 2012), 56.

9:28-36. The apostle John doesn't report the event directly. However, it has been observed that the whole of John's Gospel – that "whispering forest of all traditional poetries," as Hugh Kenner describes it – is coruscating with the transfiguration's light.

It is a moment "in and out of time" (Moses and Elijah are present) when heaven and earth meet. The splendour of God's radiance emanates from Jesus' face and clothes as the voice of God is heard to say, "This is my Son, the Beloved; listen to him" (Mark 9:7).

Initially, Peter humorously tries to capture and tame the moment with the suggestion of pitching tents, feeling perhaps how his known world has been perilously destabilized and transfigured by God's coming world. Fear and hope are mutually indistinguishable even as utter incomprehension melds with awe. Not surprisingly, the three disciples collapse onto the ground and cover their eyes and ears.

Then, just as the glory seems too much to bear, things suddenly return to "normal," and the disciples are left alone with their friend. They descend the mountain to the needy crowds where Jesus, after healing a demon-possessed child, sets his face towards Jerusalem.

When I travelled in Egypt with my friend Rikk Watts, Rikk pointed out the parallels between this story and that of the Exodus. Moses hears the cry of an oppressed people and leads them to the Red Sea, which obeys his command to let them pass before drowning legions of Pharaoh's soldiers after them. Moses then ascends a mountain where he encounters God and returns with his face shining like the sun.

Similarly, Jesus, moved by the crowds, engages in their suffering, crosses a body of water that obeys his voice, then casts a legion of demons into those same waters before ascending the mountain where his face begins to shine like the sun. The point of departure from the Exodus story is that Jesus does not just meet God on the mountain, but rather is revealed as the very God of Israel's history. He doesn't shine with the light of God. He *is* the light of God.

At this point we can better understand the terror of the disciples on the mountain, even though Christ's image is described in terms that should elevate the heart to delighted wonder and praise rather than trembling fear.

In his commentary on the Lectionary, professor Fred Gaiser describes Psalm 50 in the light of the transfiguration:

We might want to probe more deeply... the full import of coming into God's presence, of hearing God's word in its fullness. God is God, and we are not, so this is dangerous territory. The disciples were right to be terrified. It will take some figuring out to realize that this blazing fire burns only to purify, to make our robes as white as those of Jesus, to free us from our little attempts to tame God.[11]

---

11   Gaiser, "Commentary on Psalm 50:1-6."

Of course – and here's where the shadow passes over the sun and brings a certain chill to the heart – we remember that the transfiguration isn't actually the revelation of Jesus' glory. It is a revelation of his divinity. Only after this revelation does Jesus decidedly proceed to the cross at Golgotha, where his true glory is revealed – not as the self-aggrandizing pharaohs of old, or the tyrants of Rome, or the titans of Wall Street, but as the humiliated king who willingly and lovingly gives his all for his all.

It is staggering to contemplate this story. It is even more staggering to consider that in the light of Christ, we too are transfigured, revealed for who we are – beloved children of God – who are then sent down the mountain, as it were, to the world he loves, to bear witness in our own flesh to the content of this love.

BURNING EMBER

music and lyrics by Steve Bell

Judge for yourself how great is the one
Who lives in God – whose God is love
Like an iron when left in embers bright
Everything is fire – everything is light
Oh Love, how beautiful you are
Oh flame of joy within my heart

Burning ember
I remember love's first light in me
I was cold then
Like a stone when I saw your flickering
Oh what beauty as
You drew near me
I could scarcely speak
Somehow I knew
I would be new in your glowing

Judge for yourself if a fire isn't safe
When cities fall before her face
Yet a flower can endure the course of a storm
When bowing to the tempest's rage
Oh Love, more fierce than all the rest
Oh raging joy within my breast

Burning ember I remember
Love's first light in me
I was cold then
Like a stone when I saw your flickering
Burn forever
Let me never curse the pain you bring
Somehow I know
I will be whole in your burning

Oh Love, more lovely than the rest
Oh flame of joy within my breast

Burning ember
Shine forever in the darkest tomb
Warmth of heaven
Hidden secret in a mother's womb
Flame of beauty
Blazing through me so that all might see
Somehow we know
We'll all be whole in your burning

Listen to the above song at www.pilgrimyear.com/songs:
Ordinary Time Chapter Four.

5

THE FEAST OF
SAINT CLARE OF ASSISI

August 11

Our labour here is brief, but the reward is eternal. Do not be disturbed by the clamour of the world which passes like a shadow. Do not let the false delights of a deceptive world deceive you.[12]

Gaze upon Him, consider Him,
contemplate Him,
as you desire to imitate Him.[13]

Saint Clare of Assisi

12　From Clare's letter to Erentrude of Bruges, in *Francis and Clare: The Complete Works* (Paulist Press, 1982), 207.

13　From Clare's second letter to Agnes of Prague, in *Francis and Clare: The Complete Works*, 197.

I f asked who, of the ancient saints, most fully embraced holy poverty as an act of obedience and openness to God, most people would probably say, without much hesitation, Francis of Assisi. However, if you asked Francis the same question, I suspect he would answer, Clare of Assisi. And if you asked Clare, I imagine she would say, Jesus! – the "King of angels" and "Lord of heaven and earth" whose "wondrous humility" and "marvellous poverty"[14] she sincerely desired to mirror, as the moon mirrors the sun and offers light to a darkened world below.

One cannot understand the advent of Francis (1181/82–1226) and Clare (1194–1253) and those who would follow them without first knowing a little about the social context in which they lived their remarkable lives. Thirteenth-century Europe was a time of social instability and violence as the emerging merchant class began to challenge both the long-established nobility and religious institutions corrupted by power, status and wealth. The result was that families fought against families and cities warred against cities as they sought to grow and protect wealth largely acquired at the expense of the poor. As a result, many of Assisi's children, much like the children in our own day, were sickened by the gluttonous, greedy aspirations of their parents and saw no good future in continuing those behaviours.

---

14 From Clare's third letter to Agnes of Prague. *Francis and Clare: The Complete Works*, 204, 205.

Francis, who belonged to the merchant class and was famous for his youthful excesses, fought and suffered in these turf wars. Eventually, his struggles led to a physical and psychic breakdown prior to his radical conversion to the way of Christ as the way of salvation for the soul and for society. Clare belonged to the noble class and was raised in palatial privilege, although the women in her family were renowned for their piety well before she chose to dispossess all to follow Francis. Indeed, Clare's sister Catherine and mother, Ortolana, eventually joined her and were among the first members of the religious order that would come to be known as the Poor Clares. Together, Francis and Clare, differing from each other as a consequence of gender and social class, incarnated a Christ-like response to the social distemper of the day in a manner and spirit that has captured the imagination and kindled the devotion of souls in every generation since. I suspect their example and witness may, in our day, still rise to meet steep challenges unique in human history.

Little is known of Clare's story. Restricted by the social mores of the day, she and her followers didn't roam the countryside like Francis and his brothers, inspiring fantastic legends. Instead, after her dramatic nocturnal escape from the prison of her father's palace at the age of seventeen, she reluctantly submitted to the cloistered life. Eventually, she became the prioress of the monastery at San Damiano as well as the first woman in history to write a monastic rule approved by Rome.

I first encountered the story of Clare in a movie about Francis when I was a young boy. In the movie, as I recall, Claire was represented as a delicate and docile creature. She may well have been delicate and docile in her relationship to the will of God, the love of Christ and the impulses of the Spirit. But what little we know of her by legend and her own brief writings suggests an uncommon wisdom, resolve and fortitude, which she wielded against any authority that would hinder a person's primary commitment to embrace and imitate the Poor Christ in the spirit of great humility and ardent charity – even if that authority were papal authority. Clare, for example, urged Agnes of Prague, a Bohemian princess, not to comply with Pope Gregory IX's advice that she not divest herself of her wealth:

> Indeed, if someone tells you something else or suggests anything to you that may hinder your perfection and that seems contrary to your divine vocation, even though you must respect him, still, do not follow his advice; instead, poor virgin, embrace the Poor Christ.[15]

In her marvellous book *Clare of Assisi: A Heart Full of Love*, Ilia Delio explains the Franciscan appeal to poverty as a "renunciation of the instinct to power, to the dominion over things" in imitation of Christ who divested himself of his divinity in order to enter into the "fraternity of all

---

15   From Clare's second letter to Agnes of Prague, in *Francis and Clare: The Complete Works*, 197.

creation" in its utter dependence on God.[16] These remarkable saints of Assisi believed this to be a simple and sane antidote to the madness and violence that had become a feature of their world. However, Delio insists that the poverty of Francis and Clare, in imitation of Christ, is not mere renunciation for renunciation's sake, but rather the precondition for revelation. For "poverty means receptivity, and creation is intended to be the womb of God's grace."[17]

The poverty that Francis and Clare embraced was not a dour poverty but rather a joyful knowledge of the gift of creaturely existence united in common dependence on God. They rejected an understanding of creation as independent of God and each other, a view that led only to an endless war for limited resources. Clare and Francis renounced this ethic of competition and saw God's creation as calling for brotherly and sisterly cooperation.

More could be said about Clare's fascinating and inspiring life, but those details are readily available online or in various books. G.K. Chesterton's *St. Francis of Assisi* is a winsome account of Francis and the life that inspired Clare. Joan Mueller's *Clare of Assisi: The Letters to Agnes* contextualizes the four surviving letters that Clare wrote to Agnes of Prague and brings to life a dynamic moment in the history of women's spirituality. But it is an insight from Ilia Delio's *Clare of Assisi: A Heart Full of Love* that I would like to highlight before drawing this reflection to a close.

16   Ilia Delio, *Clare of Assisi: A Heart Full of Love* (Franciscan Media, 1993,) 15.
17   Delio, *Clare of Assisi*, 16.

In articulating the essence of a spirituality that can sustain the selfless love that marked Clare's life, Delio identifies four pillars in Clare's own thought that characterize her pathway to God. In her second letter to Agnes, Clare writes:

O most noble Queen,
gaze upon [him]
consider [him]
contemplate [him]
as you desire to imitate [him]

Before briefly addressing each pillar (gaze, consider, contemplate, imitate), I want to note the opening address to Agnes as "noble Queen." Notwithstanding that the letter was addressed to a specific person who held a particular social distinction, I cannot help but see the double meaning as Clare understood the dignity of our creatureliness, indeed all of creation, to be the womb of God's grace. Therefore, the letter is addressed to all those who in faith understand their royal dignity as maternal spouse of the "King of angels."

Clare encourages us to *gaze* on him; that is, on Christ, our spouse. As the moon, by rising above and looking beyond the earth, sees and reflects the sun, it becomes by grace what the sun is by nature. That is... light. This is the created dignity of every human: to look beyond our station, to gaze upon the face of our beloved and to radiate his glory. Anything less is beneath our dignity.

The fruit of gazing is the gift of *consideration*. To consider, or examine, one must first look upon what one is considering. How do we look upon and examine Christ except through the lens of the gospels? By searching the gospels, the features of the face of Christ become apparent, which the ardent gaze may then consider.

The fruit of gazing and considering is *contemplation*. Contemplation is a step deeper than consideration. In contemplation we allow the truth and beauty of the other to penetrate and transform us. Convinced by our gaze and consideration of the beauty of our Beloved, our hearts become receptive to the energies of God, whom we receive as a bride receives her bridegroom.

The fruit of the pathway thus taken is *imitation*. Not an imitation achieved by dour and dutiful effort, but rather as the joyful consequence of the holy desire awakened by our gaze, consideration and contemplation of the Poor Christ. It is love imitating Love, as the moon imitates the sun.

Thus, at the end of her life, Clare, who had suffered rejection, poverty, illness, dangers and toils that would stagger modern men and women, was wont to rhapsodize:

> Happy, indeed, is she to whom it is given to share
>   this sacred banquet,
> to cling with all her heart to Him
> Whose beauty all the heavenly hosts admire
>   unceasingly,
> Whose love inflames our love,

Whose contemplation is our refreshment,
Whose graciousness is our joy,
Whose gentleness fills us to overflowing,
Whose remembrance brings a gentle light,
Whose fragrance will revive the dead,
Whose glorious vision will be the happiness
of all the citizens of the heavenly Jerusalem.[18]

Our contemporary sensibilities recoil from the selfless austerity of saints like Clare and Francis, but our ecstasies pale as well. Given the catastrophic excesses of our time, more than ever we need the clarity and light of Clare of Assisi to bathe our imaginations with the light of Christ whom she so luminously reflects.

Shortly after her death, Pope Alexander IV proclaimed Clare a saint of the universal Church with these words:

O Clare, endowed with so many titles of Clarity! Clear (*clara*) even before your conversion, clearer (*clariour*) in your manner of living, exceedingly clear (*praeclarior*) in your enclosed life, and brilliant (*clarissima*) in splendour after the course of your mortal life. In Clare, a clear mirror is given to the entire world.[19]

---

18 From Clare's fourth letter to Agnes of Prague, *Francis and Clare: The Complete Works*, 204.
19 *Francis and Clare: The Complete Works*, 169.

In closing, I leave you with a sonnet by Malcolm Guite, whose vision, too, has been clarified by this most shining gem of Assisi's children:

CLARE

by Malcolm Guite

Santa Chiara, lovely claritas
Whose soul in stillness holds love's pure reflection,
Shining through you as Holy Caritas,
Lucid and lucent, bringing to perfection
The girl whom Love has called to call us all
Back into truth, simplicity and grace.
Your love for Francis, radiant through the veil,
Reveals in both of you your saviour's face.
Christ holds the mirror of your given life
Up to the world he gives himself to save,
A sacrament to keep your city safe,
A window into his eternal love.
Unveiled in heaven, dancing in the light,
Pray for this pilgrim soul in his dark night.[20]

---

20   Guite, *The Singing Bowl*, 81.

THE FEAST OF
SAINT FRANCIS OF ASSISI

October 4

His theme was always the same,
but the way he said it made it sound so wonderful,
so full of beauty, so new and so fresh.
It was like surging waves of love,
explosions of God-like charity![21]

Felix Timmermans

Like so many others, I was staggered on March 13, 2013, when Cardinal Jorge Mario Bergoglio was elected the 266th pope of the Roman Catholic Church and chose Francis as his papal name. When I heard the news, I felt a breeze blow through my soul that left me in a state of awe-filled silence and serene happiness.

---

21   Felix Timmermans, *The Perfect Joy of Saint Francis: A Novel* (Ignatius Press, 1952), 108.

I was not the only person who was surprised. Gregory Wolfe, editor of *Image* magazine, wrote, "Francis. The perfect name. Simplicity. Poverty. Reform. I am stunned and profoundly happy." From across the ocean, English poet Malcolm Guite also rhapsodized in a sonnet for both Saint Francis and the new pope:

FRANCIS

by Malcolm Guite

'Francis rebuild my church which, as you see
Is falling into ruin.' From the cross
Your saviour spoke to you and speaks to us
Again through you. Undoing set you free,
Loosened the traps of trappings, cast away
The trammeling of all that costly cloth
We wind our saviour in. At break of day
He set aside his grave-clothes. Your new birth
Came like a daybreak too. Naked and true
To poverty and to the gospel call,
You woke to Christ and Christ awoke in you
And set to work through all your love and skill
To make our ruin good, to bless and heal,
To wake the Christ in us and make us whole[22]

Of course, this enthusiasm is primarily associated with Saint Francis, as Jorge Mario Bergoglio's story is still being

---

22   Guite, *The Singing Bowl*, 80.

written. But the pontiff's inaugural homily gave many people cause for great hope when he presented a clear message of his vision for the Church: to work to protect God's creation and the world's poor.

However, one wonders at the wisdom of this name choice, which will now be the standard against which his life will be measured and remembered. But I think he knows this, for already, every time he breaks into the crowds to touch and be touched, he repeatedly begs, "Pray for me."

Even as this name choice could be considered courageous, it could equally be considered rash. But that is part of the charm. In an elegant biography of Francis of Assisi, G.K. Chesterton describes the man as a "festive figure" whose life was one "riot of rash vows" which turned out right.[23] A papacy marked by a riot of rash vows that turn out right is what the Church needs now. So I will not join the ranks of the cynical chic, but have decided to take the pope at his word and to do what he asks: I will pray for him.

These events sent me to my bookshelf to pull out the several books I've read on the life of Francis of Assisi. I soon found myself happily ensconced on my couch, dog in lap, rereading Chesterton's grand biography of the saint. An early sentence caught me off-guard and propelled me back into my childhood memories: "when, long ago in those days of boyhood my fancy first caught fire with the Glory of St. Francis of Assisi."[24]

---

23   G.K. Chesterton, *Saint Francis of Assisi* (Doubleday, 1957), 42.
24   Chesterton, *Saint Francis of Assisi*, 17.

I was in Grade 2 or 3 when, having just returned home from school, my sisters and I were surprised by Mom and Dad with the news that we would make the 60-mile trek to Calgary that evening to see a movie. It's not that there wasn't a theatre in our little town of Drumheller, Alberta; rather, in those days movie going was frowned upon by "the faithful." To avoid scandal, the few movies I saw as a boy were always preceded by a clandestine journey.

You might imagine how my initial excitement was dashed to learn that the movie we were about to see was called *Brother Sun, Sister Moon*, which told the story of a thirteenth-century saint named Francis. I would have much preferred something involving a car chase, a heroic battle scene or, more secretly, a romance involving a buxom beauty. But alas, it was already risqué enough that we Baptists would engage a dubious Catholic legend.

That being said, my disappointment was soon over-turned. The cinematography, story and music (by Scottish singer/songwriter Donovan, no less) overwhelmed me and became one of my earliest remembered spiritual experien-ces. I knew I was encountering something utterly *beyond*. From that day on, when some kindly man or woman would ask me what I hoped to be when I grew up, I would boyishly answer policeman, fireman, etc. The truth that I was too shy to tell was that I really wanted to be a saint.

Soon after, we learned to sing a prayer attributed to Francis:

Lord, make me an instrument of your peace,
Where there is hatred, let me sow love;
Where there is injury, pardon;
Where there is doubt, faith;
Where there is despair, hope;
Where there is darkness, light;
Where there is sadness, joy.

O Divine Master,
grant that I may not so much seek to be consoled,
as to console;
to be understood, as to understand;
to be loved, as to love.
For it is in giving that we receive.
It is in pardoning that we are pardoned,
and it is in dying that we are born to eternal life.

I realize now how deeply those words have seeped into my being and shaped my understanding. What a gift!

Years later, a friend was waiting backstage after a concert to shove a book into my hands before she ran to catch a ride home. It was entitled *Love Poems from God,* a book of mystical poetry edited by Daniel Ladinsky, which includes several obscure poems attributed to Francis. One, in particular, took my breath away, and a song soon followed, which I leave you with to commemorate this day, the Feast of Saint Francis.

May we, like Francis, be fertile ground for the seed of Christ, and a new flowering of love and grace in our own day.

EVER PRESENT NEED

by Steve Bell (lyrics adapted from Daniel Ladinski's translation of "Our Need for Thee" in Love Poems from God. *Original poem attributed to Saint Francis of Assisi.)*

Darkness is an unlit wick
A simple spark would vanquish it
Truly I could burst to flame
Every time you call my name
Do I do for you the same?

God is like a honey bee
Penetrates the soul of me
Dearly draws the sweetness in
Nectar of the meek love is
He in me and I in him

In our ever present need of thee
Grant we fathom peace
Fashion instruments of souls set free
For don't the caged ones weep

Sometimes sober sometimes bliss
Every union knows of this
But I have stood here in his rain

And bear the marks of fertile plains
Swelling streams and swollen grain

So will I console the fall
Of cheerless creatures great and small
What of sadness can endure
When love divine makes insecure
The crowing claims of shame's allure?

Listen to the above song at pilgrimyear.com/songs: Ordinary Time Chapter Six.

ALLHALLOWMAS TRIDUUM

October 31 – November 2

O Almighty God, who hast knit together thine
elect in one communion and fellowship, in the
mystical body of thy Son Christ our Lord;
Grant us grace so to follow thy blessed Saints
in all virtuous and godly living,
that we may come to those unspeakable
joys, which thou hast prepared for them that
unfeignedly love thee;
through Jesus Christ our Lord. Amen.[25]

Collect for All Saints (Thomas Cranmer)

very year, the Western Church sets aside three days
(in Latin: *triduum*) to remember the dead and commemorate the communion of saints – the holy (hallowed)

25   Collect for the Feast of All Saints, in *Book of Common Prayer* (Oxford
University Press, 1979).

ones. These days are All Hallows' Eve, All Saints' Day and All Souls' Day.

During this time, we recall with humility and deep gratitude that others have gone before us on whose shoulders we now stand; the faith we profess is inherited and comes to us as a gift from generation after generation of faithful souls who persevered in love so we might do the same. We also reflect on the mystery of death as passage to greater, verdant life, and we ponder with awe the mystery of our communion in Christ. That communion assures us that those who have already made the passage are ever-present to us, and we to them. We celebrate with great joy that *love* wins, even as we grieve the felt separation that our dimmed vision perceives.

The first Christians instinctively remembered and celebrated heroes of the faith. These heroes were the early saints whose lives and deaths were uniquely graced to give witness to the love of God. They energized and re-energized faith and courage in others, especially in those early dark days when fidelity to Christ often cost a person their life. Martyrs, in particular, were remembered annually on the day of their deaths, which became yearly festivals. Over time there became too many martyrs for each to have their own day, so in the early sixth century a single day – All Saints' Day, or Hallowmas, with its accompanying vigil, All Hallows' Eve (Halloween) – was established to celebrate them all. Later, in the eleventh century, a third day was added to commemorate not just the martyrs, but all the faithful departed with whom we are eternally united in Christ.

Allhallowmas is a rich and meaningful tradition.

Here I would like to point out with some bemusement that certain Christian groups in recent times have rejected the tradition of Halloween (kids dressing up and going from house to house for candy) on the basis that it is a satanic festival. In fact, its very name (hallow, which means 'holy') should indicate the opposite. The confusion arises in that All Hallows' Eve falls on the same night as the pagan Celtic festival of Samhain, when it was believed that the veil between the dead and the living was, for one night, so thin that the dead could cross over to the realm of the living. This created fear that some of those souls might be malevolent, bearing grudges from their living years. The Celts would mask themselves so as to be unrecognizable and place gourds carved with frightening faces in their windows in an attempt to scare away the vengeful marauding souls. It was a terrifying night for most.

But the early Christians (it is thought perhaps Saint Patrick himself) went out boldly in the night, giving sweets and cakes to their neighbours, announcing that we need not fear the dead, but rather are called to celebrate and honour them. In Christ the veil is thin indeed, and we already enjoy a tremendous fellowship and communion with the eternally redeemed.

When we huddle in fear against the night, we more closely represent the poor Celts than the hallowed ones whose joy and faith inspired them to do the opposite.

This is relevant to our day. We live in increasingly desperate times. People are afraid. Our horror at the thought of death results in fortress-minded social trends and policies that cut us off from one another; ironically, these produce the very death (separation) we are most afraid of. By attending mindfully to the Allhallowmas Triduum, we may reanimate our gospel joy and courage for living in death's shadow. And it is indeed a mere shadow – a phantom of no substance in the light of Christ's death-conquering love and the witness of his saints.

One dark night, years ago, my young sons were playing hockey on our homemade rink in the backyard. I sat in my study reading, while the muffled clacking of sticks and the slice and swoosh of skates played like a happy song from my own youth. The boys, as boys do, were loudly offering their own hockey commentary, as well as the roar of the crowd with each goal.

After a while I noticed that the sounds had stopped, but I hadn't heard the boys come in the house. I went to the window to see what they were up to, and there they were, lying on their backs on the ice with chests rising and falling to produce white puffs of air with each breath. They were both gazing silently into the stars, which were myriad and gazing back on them. I suddenly perceived with my heart's eye that these stars were the kind and blinking eyes of the saints looking down on my boys with great delight. I wanted to run outside, yelling, "Play on! Play on, sons! You have fans! Play on!"

Only a few months afterward, in the late summer, I was sitting by a quiet lake in the evening. The low sun was setting the surface of the water on fire with a billion facets of light reflecting its beauty. Again, I was suddenly graced to perceive those blazing facets as kindly blinking eyes. I knew I was not alone as I simply received their gaze and blinked back in deep and grateful friendship.

DIAMONDS FROM THE OTHER SIDE

music by Steve Bell

lyrics by Steve Bell and Carolyn Arends

From August shores and summers past
Low sun fire on the liquid glass
From facets on the surface of the bay

Burns the beauty deep inside
Returning when I close my eyes
To find me when I'm time and miles away
Calling me back again

Almost too much for human eyes
Diamonds from the other side

Deep the heavens – deep the dark
That hide the earth to show the spark
Of stars that wait on the other side of day

Now you see them – now you don't
Regardless of the clouds you know
To close your eyes and there they are again
Holding you in their gaze

Almost too much for human eyes
Diamonds from the other side

*Listen to the above song at www.pilgrimyear.com/songs:
Ordinary Time Chapter Seven.*

THE FEAST OF CHRIST THE KING

Last Sunday of Ordinary Time

The Feast of Christ the King is the last Sunday of the Western Church's calendar year before we start all over, rehearsing (reharrowing) the great gospel story that begins with the preparatory season of Advent.

To commemorate this feast, Malcolm Guite wrote a beautiful, unsettling sonnet riffing off of today's gospel reading in Matthew (25:31-46), which anticipates the day when Christ the King, upon *coming in glory*, will ask us whether we recognized him in the poor, the marginalized, the hungry, the thirsty.

Before reading the sonnet, it is worth carefully reading and reflecting on the passage:

When the Son of Man comes in his glory, and all the angels with him, then he will sit on the throne of his glory. All the nations will be gathered before him, and he will separate people one from another as a shepherd separates the sheep from the goats, and he will put the sheep at his right hand and the goats at the left.

Then the king will say to those at his right hand, "Come, you that are blessed by my Father, inherit the kingdom prepared for you from the foundation of the world; for I was hungry and you gave me food, I was thirsty and you gave me something to drink, I was a stranger and you welcomed me, I was naked and you gave me clothing, I was sick and you took care of me, I was in prison and you visited me."

Then the righteous will answer him, "Lord, when was it that we saw you hungry and gave you food, or thirsty and gave you something to drink? And when was it that we saw you a stranger and welcomed you, or naked and gave you clothing? And when was it that we saw you sick or in prison and visited you?"

And the king will answer them, "Truly I tell you, just as you did it to one of the least of these who are members of my family, you did it to me." (Matthew 25:31-40)

Rev. Dr. Randy Woodley, in his fine book *Shalom and the Community of Creation: An Indigenous Vision*, suggests that it may well be time for us to drop the language of *king* and *kingdom* from our Christian lexicon, as the metaphor no longer has direct relevance in our modern context and is also freighted with negative associations.

While Woodley's concerns resonate with me, the tension between ruler and ruled is precisely the point of this feast. Exactly what kind of king is this who volunteers obscurity, who condescends (with passion) to walk among the lowly, sharing their burdens and humiliations, and whose rule paradoxically accomplishes the liberation rather than the oppressive servitude of his subjects?

What kind of kingdom is it where the lofty are brought down and the lowly lifted up, where the marginalized are brought into the centre, where the weak are heralded as its prized citizens?

This passage describes an odd, counter-intuitive sort of kingdom and kingly glory, does it not? The sort that modern scientism, famously articulated by Thomas Sprat of the English Royal Society in 1667, claims can perhaps only be found in "the delightful deceits of fables." But I'll take those so-called *deceits* any day over the relentlessly measured, flat, atomized facts of a pitiless universe where domination supplants dominion, where authoritarianism is mistaken for authority, and where power is leveraged for personal aggrandizement and preferred to self-giving love.

Jesus radically redefined the nature of kingship when he said, "Whoever wishes to become great among you must be your servant, and whoever wishes to be first among you must be slave of all. For the Son of Man came not to be served but to serve, and to give his life a ransom for many" (Mark 10:43-45).

I truly love, believe and trust this story of the servant king and his upside-down kingdom. It causes me to weep tears of both awe and shame. I am complicit in the structures and systems that allow for wretchedness to exist alongside historically unprecedented privilege. Yet, what makes me get up in the morning, dust off my shame and jump back into the story is the firm conviction that the story isn't over. My belief and hope is that the Author, whose astonishing glory is embedded and foreshadowed in countless previous chapters of world history, may yet have a surprise ending.

Below you'll find Malcolm's sonnet for Christ the King. While reading, consider the irony that the feast to commemorate this almost unimaginable king and kingdom follows close on the heels of the secular consumer high holiday known as Black Friday, a modern orgiastic festival of unrestrained consumerism.

Lastly, I've offered a song, "High Above the Fray," taken from Psalm 113, which echoes Malcolm's insights and voices a deep love and longing for *the return of the king…* which is precisely the point of Advent.

CHRIST THE KING

by Malcolm Guite

Our King is calling from the hungry furrows
Whilst we are cruising through the aisles of plenty,
Our hoardings screen us from the man of sorrows,
Our soundtracks drown his murmur: 'I am thirsty'.
He stands in line to sign in as a stranger
And seek a welcome from the world he made,
We see him only as a threat, a danger,
He asks for clothes, we strip-search him instead.
And if he should fall sick then we take care
That he does not infect our private health,
We lock him in the prisons of our fear
Lest he unlock the prison of our wealth.
But still on Sunday we shall stand and sing
The praises of our hidden Lord and King.[26]

---

26   Guite, *Sounding the Seasons*, 62.

HIGH ABOVE THE FRAY

by Steve Bell (adapted from Psalm 113)

From the rising of the sun
To the setting of the same
Who is like the one who is our maker
Every citizen belongs
To a nation and a name
But high above these things is their keeper

Blessed be the name of the Lord
My heart pounds out this praise
Let every weary doubter be assured
It is He! High above the fray!

And he picks up from the dust
Every lost and lowly wretch
Inviting them to come to the table
And he honours them among
The brightest and the best
Who could have guessed?
No one is able

Blessed be the name of the Lord
My heart pounds out this praise
Let every weary doubter be assured
It is He! High above the fray!

*Listen to the above song at www.pilgrimyear.com/songs:
Ordinary Time Chapter Eight.*

Epilogue

SANCTUS BENEDICTUS:
HOLY AND BLESSED

I t seems fitting to end this book series with the *Sanctus Benedictus* (*Sanctus* meaning 'holy'; *Benedictus* meaning 'blessed'), which the Church sings week after week, recalling the prophet Isaiah's vision of heaven where the six-winged angels spiral in ecstatic flight around the throne of God, calling out to one another:

> "Holy, Holy, Holy is the Lord Almighty;
> The whole earth is full of [God's] glory."
> (Isaiah 6:3; NIV)

Readers of these pages will have noticed how often I've quoted the poetry of Malcolm Guite. I would like to thank Malcolm here for permission to use his poems, but more so for writing them. Indeed, his collection *Sounding the Seasons: Seventy Sonnets for the Christian Year* (Canterbury Press, 2012) captured my imagination several years ago and sparked a fire that was to become this series. Malcolm closes his volume with a sonnet called "Sanctus." In deference to the profound impact of his work on me, I want to close with his sonnet as well as a Sanctus of my own.

Malcolm once told me the inspiration for this poem. He was performing at Greenbelt Music Festival in England one summer. On one serene afternoon he was resting on the grass while the wind carried and bathed him with the sublime music of Mozart's *Requiem* from some distant stage. Requiems, of course, are for the dead, many of whom have been celebrated in these pages. "Such music," Malcolm writes, "must have an element of yearning and longing, since we sing for those we have lost, and since all the best and even the most joyful of the songs of the earth have that elegiac note of exile and yearning for home, but it must also have an element of joy and mystery, since it echoes the joy and music of heaven."

SANCTUS

by Malcolm Guite

We gather as his Church on God's good earth
And listen to the Requiem's intense,
Long, love-laden keening, calling forth
Echoes of Eden, blessing every sense
With brimming blisses, every death with birth,
Until all passion passes into praise.
I bless the hidden threads that drew us here,
I bless this day, distinct amidst our days,

I bless the light, the music laden air,
I bless the interweaving of our days,
The lifting of the burdens that we bear,
I bless the broken body that we share.
Sanctus the heart, *Sanctus* the spirit cries,
Sanctus the flesh in every touch replies.

Malcolm's sonnet touches on the reality of the thin veil between heaven and earth suggested by the many festivals and traditions that the Christian calendar tradition preserves and rehearses year after year. Notwithstanding the grim reality of sin and the terrible suffering it wreaks upon the earth and its inhabitants, the angels still sing, "The whole earth is full of God's glory," and our tradition asserts that a good God has not abandoned, and will not abandon, his (very) good creation.

Native American wisdom teacher Marcus Briggs-Cloud (Maskoke Nation), in his essay "Return to the Good," writes that "it is time for us to reclaim our Genesis," but that "we must intimately interact with what is 'good' in order to effectively enact what is good."[27] My own experience of attending to the seasons has revitalized my hope and my faith that I, too, imperfect as I am, in concert with the angels and the saints, may participate meaningfully in this holy enactment of the good, which God will redeem and bring to completion in the fullness of time.

---

27 Steve Heinrichs, *Unsettling the Word: Biblical Experiments in Decolonization* (Common Word, 2018), 6.

What I have written in this series is not the work of a priest or scholar, and doesn't pretend to do much more than document a layman's insights into a rich and ever-green tradition. The reflections are not so much to direct the reader's experience as to stimulate a devotional interest in a narrative tradition that has fuelled humanity's better instincts for centuries. It has been good for me to write them. I hope they have been good to read.

THE WELLSPRING

music and lyrics by Steve Bell

The Father gives away his word and his breath
And all things are called into being
This mystery of love and of life is a gift
And its glory beyond human reason

And Holy, Holy, Holy is
The God of power and might
In all of heaven and earth
His glory lives
Hosanna in the Highest
Hosanna in the Highest

Whatever he speaks is worthy to be
Pure and blameless and holy
Whatever he speaks is lovely indeed
Forever reflecting his glory

And Holy, Holy, Holy is
The God of power and might
In all of heaven and earth
His glory lives
Hosanna in the Highest
Hosanna in the Highest

HOLY LORD (SANCTUS, BENEDICTUS)

by Steve Bell

Holy, Holy, Holy Lord
God of power and might
Heaven and earth of your glory are full
Hosanna! Hosanna! Hosanna in the highest!

Blessed is he who comes in the name of the Lord
Blessed is he who comes in the name of the Lord

Listen to the above songs at pilgrimyear.com/songs:
Ordinary Time Epilogue.

THANKS

The first iteration of this project began as a multimedia e-book series for which I am indebted and grateful to Troubadour Media (Jim Richardson, Jim Van Eerden and Tim Krupa) for direction and practical support. Amy Knight coordinated the project, read and edited first drafts, and worked with Kelly Milne to edit the final draft. Fr. Jamie Howison read the early drafts and offered helpful and insightful suggestions for the project's betterment.

I am most grateful to Glen Argan, who brought the project to the attention of Novalis Publishing, which has resulted in Pilgrim Year being published in traditional book form.

Much has been reworked and rewritten for this second iteration of Pilgrim Year. Thank you to Glen Argan and Anne Louise Mahoney, whose gentle edits massaged the text into readable form. Thank you also to Joseph Sinasac and Simon Appolloni at Novalis for such kind enthusiasm and encouragement.

Many thanks to Roberta Landreth, who created the wonderful design elements for the book cover, and to my songwriting friends who graciously consented to my reprinting their lyrics and posting their songs on the companion website: Gord Johnson, Alana (Levandoski) Porteous, Jim Croegaert, Bob Bennett, Glen Soderholm, Ken Medema, Mary Gautier and John Foley.

The series was initially inspired by the poetry of Malcolm Guite, especially his elegant volume *Sounding the Seasons: Seventy Sonnets for the Christian Year*. Thank you to Canterbury Press for allowing us to reprint many of Malcolm's poems here.

My manager/business partner, Dave Zeglinski, has been my champion and dearest friend for nearly thirty years. Our staff – Faye Hall, Amy Knight and Don Betts – have been a dream team; I couldn't hope to work with finer people. My advisory board, Jim Richardson, Ren Martens, David Jennings and Uli Chi, have been invaluable friends and sounding boards at key points of discernment over the years.

My parents, Alfred and Marie Bell, have been steadfast champions my entire life and taught me by example to be an earnest and honest seeker after God. My dear wife, Nanci, has been a loving, long-suffering and steady support throughout all my endeavours.

Pilgrim Year is a series of reflections that only scratches the surface of a rich Christian tradition. I wrote it as part of my own discovery, but also with the hope of enticing readers to attend, perhaps a little deeper, to what the Church has to offer by way of this treasury of feasts, fasts and remembrances which water and nourish the Christian mind, body and soul. I enjoyed the work and I share it knowing full well that so much more could have been much better said.

ABOUT THE AUTHOR

Canadian Christian singer/songwriter Steve Bell is a modern-day troubadour whose vocal style, rootsy guitar riffs and storytelling prowess have won him concerts the world over. Increasingly, he is being invited to teach on Christian faith and practice at conferences and university campuses across Canada and the United States.

His work has garnered a stream of accolades, including three JUNO Awards; multiple Western Canadian Music Association and Gospel Music Association Covenant Awards; and the Queen Elizabeth ll Diamond Jubilee Medal for his commitment to artistic excellence, social activism and advocacy work. Having independently released twenty albums, three concert videos, and five songbooks, Steve is now turning his energies towards devotional writing.

After a storied lifetime of contribution to the Canadian music industry, Steve remains compelled to express his Christian faith and art in the wider context of bounty and need. As such, he has worked with various organizations to attract attention, build informed awareness and foster allies for the world's less fortunate and under-resourced – locally, nationally and internationally – represented by such organizations as Canadian Foodgrains Bank, World Vision and Compassion Canada. He is also passionate about and engaged with the cause of Indigenous/settler justice and reconciliation in Canada.

In addition to his year-round touring schedule, Steve has written numerous articles for various online and print publications. In all his endeavours, he remains committed to *refreshing Christian faith and spiritual tradition for the weary and the wary.*

Steve lives with his wife, Nanci, in Winnipeg, Treaty 1 Territory and homeland of the Red River Métis Nation.